IT'S ALL AN ILLUSION

IT'S ALL AN ILLUSION

by

william a. guillory

Request for such permission should be addressed to:

    Uni★Sun
    P.O. Box 25421
    Kansas City, MO 64119

This book is manufactured in the United States of America. Cover art by Leonard Parkin and distribu-tion by The Talman Company.

    The Talman Company, Inc.
    150 Fifth Avenue
    New York, N.Y. 10011

ISBN # 0-912949-11-2
LCCN: 87-051685

Uni★Sun
BOOK

To Linda

IT'S ALL AN ILLUSION

Foreword

The source of the inspiration for and content of this book is my personal mentor, Cameron. It is a story about a young college student who is mentored by an old man in discovering what is illusion and what is reality. This story is presented as an invitation to reconsider most of what we take for granted as being reality. I consider this book to be a shared experience that may provoke your thinking in such a way that you also have personal realizations.

William A. Guillory
April, 1988

Author's Preface

A consistently frustrating aspect of consciousness evolution is the use of logic to rationalize the illogical.

PREFACE

Several weeks after the old man had gone (and supposedly returned to his family), I was awakened by a persistent feeling inside which caused me to twist and turn for several hours. I finally got up, and without purpose, wandered over to my desk where partially-solved physics homework problems were strewn in disarray. I cleaned my desk in the usual way (by putting everything on the desk on the bed) and placed before me several sheets of paper. This didn't make sense, since what I should be doing was my physics homework.

The time of the morning, 2:00 a.m., wasn't at all unusual because I do my clearest thinking in the early morning hours. I think it's because both my mind and body are in a rested and relaxed state. Although I was perfectly aware and conscious, the sequence of events were somehow different although not weird or unnatural. I instinctively took the pen in my hand and it began writing. I wrote continuously for about forty-five minutes with no hesitation or second thoughts about what was being written. When I was finished, I went back to bed.

When I awakened the next morning, I wandered over to the desk, while trying to remove the cobwebs from my head. I picked up the pages of writing I had scribbled on the previous night and began reading with astonishment.

Everything that exists (past, present, and future) are all forms of dynamical energy exchanges.

Man's vision of life and descriptions are all illusions and used only as guiding principles; true existence can only be experienced and not described.

Oneness is the essential realization.

Space, time, and other dimensions are all non-existent illusions of man's mind; there is only oneness of everything there ever was, is, or will be.

There is no passage in time, since time itself is an illusion. Once you see this, really see this, you see it all.

Mankind has been fooled by his own mind to believe there was a beginning. There is, was, and never will be any beginning. Only Now! Everything! All at Once!

Life, mind, universe, however big you can think, is only mind itself.

To own something is to own nothing. To own nothing is to own (be) everything. It's an illusion to think (believe) that you own anything.

Man's reality is a figment of his (rich) imagination. There is no reality in thoughts or expression, only more thoughts expressed in more sophisticated form that displace the previous way of thinking. Therefore, man can really "never" know reality.

Reality is an all encompassing manifestation of the

universal oneness, without form, having infinite dimension; an infinity of consciousness.

Therefore, truth, like knowledge simply is, all at once and is complete. When you live life naturally, you call forth your knowledge from being natural. This ever expanding knowledge is what is called self-awareness or consciousness evolution.

Knowledge is. Beliefs are ego constructs of man's mind. Beliefs precede knowledge through the transformation process.

The extent to which one obtains wisdom is the extent to which one transcends one's ego.

This is the essential key: "all is one, (and) one is all." Realize this statement and no books are necessary.

Look deeply within yourself; there is infinite wisdom.

I had no idea what most of it meant and I was not really sure I wanted to find out either. Somehow, I had this uneasy feeling that it might have something to do with the old man. His magician-like appearance and disappearance from my life had left me thinking "Did that really happen? How about a replay?"

The only evidence that I have that something truly significant happened (like being teleported to another planet and back) is the realization of illusions in my life. These realizations have literally changed everything. Maybe what I ought to do is fill you in from the beginning.

Chapter 1

The ability of man to manipulate nature has come through unique relationships certain individuals have had with nature in a moment of oneness.

The moment of "seeing" the whole in relationship with nature is knowledge (as wisdom); the subsequent communication in any form is pure illusion.

CHAPTER 1

As I awakened that fateful morning, thinking of the meeting I was to have with the old man, I was both anxious and excited. Anxious because he always came up with the unexpected which I didn't understand, didn't want to understand, and always found confusing. I think he took delight in my confusion. Our meetings, however, had a strange fascination and attraction which I did not comprehend fully. This particular morning I felt unusually apprehensive, like the premonitions my grandma used to speak of.

I was excited because I sensed that something truly different was going to happen this time. All of our previous meetings had left me numb and confused, and ultimately with a completely different view of some of my most basic assumptions about reality. Nevertheless, I told him I would be there and I prided myself on keeping my word.

I drove out into the Louisiana countryside for what seemed like an eternity. It was only 40 miles northwest of New Orleans in a rural community forgotten by time, and most of mankind, for that matter. When I arrived, about 8:45 a.m., he was there on his dilapidated wooden porch looking into space as usual. Even though I waved, he only responded by lifting his eyebrows, as if even that took supreme effort on his part. I bounded up to him and said, "Well, I'm here, only fifteen minutes late. You know how it is with traffic and all, the city is simply get-

ting too big for its britches." He nodded impercepti-
bly and told me to sit down a minute and gather my
thoughts.

We both sat there for about fifteen minutes,
gathering our thoughts, when I finally spoke up and
said, "Are you feeling okay, old man?" He was staring off into space, wet-eyed and sad. Then he
quickly turned to me with a wide grin and said,
"It's all an illusion you know."

I said, "What?"

He repeated, "It's all an illusion."

"What is?" I said.

"Everything," he said.

"Everything?"

"Yes, what you think you see and believe isn't
real."

"Well, what is real?" I asked.

"I don't know!" he said. "I have the same problem you do! But what you think and see, definitely
isn't real."

I had suspected for some time that the old man
was leaving us, but this was as far out as he had
ever been. Sometimes I wondered why I began this
strange relationship in the first place.

My thoughts went back to our first meeting in
the New Orleans market place near the river front.
I was wandering around the market trying to get
some idea for a good Creole dinner—perhaps crabs,
okra, shrimp. What spices would I need? I didn't
notice the old man behind me as I quickly turned to
go back to the vegetable stand I had passed. When I
knocked him down, everything he had went flying
all over the street. The old man looked distraught. I
began to apologize, particularly when the crowd
looked at me accusingly.

As we gathered his groceries, I asked if he was

okay. He said, "Yes." I loudly offered to drive him home. This pleased the crowd and they began to disburse. He said no, that he was fine and could get home quite well without my assistance. For the first time, amidst all this confusion, I looked into the old man's eyes. There was an instant flicker of recognition, a knowingness, even an expectation on his part. He seemed to have run my "life film" in that instant. He grinned and asked me to help him up.

At this point, I insisted on driving him home. He simply said okay and we started toward my car. As we walked, I could hardly keep up with him. He asked me what I was studying in college.

"Physics," I told him. "How did you know I was in college?"

He went into his wide grin again, as if he knew everything, and said, "I guessed."

Somehow I had the uneasy feeling that this old man was enjoying playing mental games with me. He didn't seem so helpless or old after all; or maybe he was beyond age.

When we got to my car, I asked him where he lived.

"La Roche."

"La Roche? Where is that?"

"About forty miles northwest of New Orleans."

"Forty miles!" I exclaimed.

"You insisted on driving me home," he said, as he settled easily into the front seat of my car. "I was quite content to take the bus, as I always do." Again he looked at me twinkled-eyed with his wide grin and said, "Let's go."

Since I was stuck with the old man and our trip to La Roche, I decided to make the best of it. I asked him the usual non-question questions, about how long had he lived there, did he like it, why did he shop in New Orleans. Then he just stopped answering my questions. I thought maybe he was hard of hearing at first, and then I noticed he had his eyes closed as if he were asleep.

About a half hour later, he awakened abruptly and said, "Turn off at the sign to Parkersville, about a half mile further." How did he know to awaken a half mile before the turn off? This old man was beginning to act like somebody from the Twilight Zone. I smiled to myself at the thought.

He said, "I seem strange to you, don't I?"

Christ, even my thoughts aren't private. I couldn't wait to dump this old man and make it back to the sanity of the big city. "No," I stammered, "just a bit eccentric."

Then he said, "Take a right turn up ahead, then turn left at the silo about four miles further, and La Roche will be directly in front of us." He closed his eyes again and went back to sleep.

After following his instructions, I came to a stop in the middle of a corn field half a mile from an old stately post-Reconstruction house.

"Where's La Roche? I must have missed a turn."

"No," he said, "that's it dead ahead."

"You mean that old house is the whole town?"

"Yes, I incorporated it myself," he said with the twinkle and grin.

This old man is definitely weird. I better get the hell back to New Orleans before something else happens, I thought to myself.

"Don't be in such a rush," he said. "Have a cool drink before you start back to New Orleans."

"Okay," I said. He went inside and returned with a tall glass of lemonade. "Do you enjoy your studies in physics?"

"Yes, I do. The reason I enjoy the natural sciences, and physics in particular, is that I learn how nature and the universe operate."

"How do you do that?" he asked with an interested look.

I could see this was going to be difficult. What did he know of physics or anything for that matter, living out here in Nowheresville? "Oh, we study theories and laws of natural phenomena and even recent research results in order to get closer to the truth of how nature operates."

The old man looked confused and perplexed and asked could I help him understand what I had just said. "I always thought that theories and laws were concepts made up by scientists to explain or describe what happens in nature," the old man said.

I patiently explained to him that laws and theories not only explained and described physical phenomena, but that they could also *predict* occurrences that happened in nature or experiments.

He scratched his head momentarily and asked, "Well, do they explain, describe, and predict forever?"

"No, as we perform more sophisticated experiments, they need to be refined."

He was obviously confused again and I felt like dropping the subject all together and going on to a discussion he felt more at home with.

Then he asked, "Why do you have to refine the truth?"

"What I said was that the laws and theories of the natural sciences were about getting *closer* to the truth of how nature operates; that's why we continue to do research."

"How do you get closer to the truth? I always thought the truth was the truth," the old man said. "Perhaps I'm too simple-minded. Do you mean that your laws and theories will ultimately be refined into the truth?"

"Ultimately yes," I blurted out, not knowing what I was talking about.

"I see," he said, appearing to be satisfied.

I started having the feeling again that the old man was leading me into a trap, particularly when he twinkled and grinned. "Well," I said, "you've raised some interesting points for me to give thought to. Perhaps I'll be driving this way again and I'll stop in to see how you're doing."

"Sure!" he said. "Stop anytime."

As I drove back to the city, I couldn't forget what the old man had said about theories and laws being concepts. Certainly physical phenomena are not concepts. Then concepts and things that happen in nature are different.

I guess I really don't know for sure that particles called electrons exist in the way I've been taught, let alone atoms. I do believe *something* exists and maybe I can never really know. After all, nobody has ever *seen* an electron or an atom.

When I really think about it from this perspective, *we* devise experiments to have an electron be a particle or a wave. *If* nature is simply as it is and consistent, then how can it be both a particle and a wave? I guess it really isn't both, or maybe it isn't really either one. Maybe I'm simply creating my own reality by how I choose to examine and characterize nature.

This was all happening too fast for me, so I simply decided to shut down and forget the old man. I had taken him home and everything was just fine.

That night, as I lay in bed staring at the ceiling, I couldn't quite make sense of all the old man had said and done. I just couldn't seem to let go of the connection or non-connection between concepts and physical phenomena. Finally, I gave up, too exhausted to try anymore. Then it hit me like a bolt: the measurement; the probe; the *experience* of the physical phenomenon. That's the connection! They are all different and not one and the same.

The physical phenomenon occurs, we measure or record it by some means, and based on the measurement or recording, we interpret and conceptualize it. That's it! Each of these stages is separate and distinct. I had always assumed they were superimposed or continuously related. That's how I have always been taught: experiment, experience, and concept all presented simultaneously with no clear distinction made between the various separations. They all fit so well, I've always accepted the resulting concept as being the truth. Therefore, if there is any truth, it would have to be in the physical phenomenon or the experiment, whether we can ever know it or not.

Basically, there is no truth in science, there are only concepts derived from our experience of experiments!

So an electron in its microscopic way simply exists and our attempts to measure, examine, or manipulate it are *not* a true examination of it, but a way of *interacting* with it. There is no continuity between that called an electron and our measurements.

Furthermore, there is really no unique continuity between our measurements and the way we interpret our measurements. Probably, examining the same measurements, we could, and do, interpret them in many different ways. So that the measurement is an experience of the experiment and dependent on how we are predisposed to see it.

This can't be. Because physics is the study of reality; or that's what I've always thought and nobody ever told me any differently. I was really exhausted and confused by now and I decided it would all be better in the morning. This was just another dream, including the old man, and by morning I would wake up to reality again.

Chapter 2

*What you see is not what is there. It is simply a
thought about what is there created by the mind for
its enjoyment; an illusion in thought.*

By now you know that didn't happen. If anything, I awoke with greater clarity than ever before about physics being the study of concepts that *correlate* with reality.

This realization was both exciting and somewhat scary, since I had no idea where this might lead my thinking and exploration.

However, at that moment, I was simply too excited about my discovery and what the implications might be.

On my way back to La Roche that same morning, I couldn't wait to tell the old man about my realization. When I arrived, he met me at the stairs and said how delighted he was to see me again so soon.

"Something very strange happened to me last night," I said.

"What was that?" he asked.

"I realized for the first time that theories and laws are not only transitory but are also non-unique; that they are only *one* conceptual way of describing natural events within certain limits and not *the* only way; and then we must devise additional concepts to support the original ones or discard the entire thing and start over again."

The old man just sat there staring off into space, as usual. After about three minutes I said, "What do you think?"

"About what?" he said.

Here we go again, I said to myself. "About what I just said."

"Fine."

"Is that all you have to say?"

"Yes, what do you want me to say?"

"Do you agree or disagree?" I asked.

"Neither," he replied. "Why do you need my agreement or disagreement? I understood what you said and it's fine." The old man abruptly stood up and said, "Let's go for a walk." After walking through the thick brush for about five minutes, he said, "Do you see that yellow flower over there?"

"Of course I see it," I said.

"Is it different from you?"

Christ, here we go again, I thought to myself. I just stared at him wanting to make sure I understood his question. "Am I different from that yellow flower?" I repeated.

"Yes," he said, "that's what I asked." The twinkle and grin indicated he knew something I didn't.

"Of course, I'm different!" I said.

"How do you know you're different?" he asked.

Okay, I thought, I'll go along with his silly game. "I can *see* that it's different from me; I can touch, smell, and even taste it, to know that it's different from me."

"So, you know differences by experiences using your senses?" he asked.

"Yes," I said. "Do you know a better way?"

He smiled again and said, "No." After walking quietly for another ten minutes or so, the old man said, "How do you know you've had an experience?"

"What?"

"How do you know, you've had an experience?" he repeated.

"If I see something, like the yellow flower, my

mind instantly interprets it for me, as yellow flower, based upon previous experiences," I said intelligently.

"Let me see if I understand you," he said with his usual grin. "How do you see the yellow flower?"

I looked at him patiently and said, "Light rays reflected by the flower are collected on the retina of my eyes, and are in turn transmitted to my brain, which allows my perception of the image of a flower."

"Do you see the flower or the image?" he asked.

I started getting that feeling again, especially when the twinkle and the smile came together.

"I see the flower, of course," I answered, but feeling very uneasy. "In fact, to confirm my observation I can touch it, smell it, and even eat it, if I cared to."

The old man laughed unrestrained at my explanation. We walked past a swampy area which appeared to contain an infinite array of plant and animal life and the old man said, "Let's sit down for a minute." After looking at the swamp for about three minutes with a blank expression, he asked quizzically, "Is the signal that goes from your retina to your brain in the form of a flower?"

"No," I said patiently, "it's an electrical signal which is collected by my brain and subsequently interpreted by my mind; it generates the image, 'yellow flower.' "

"So do you see the image or the real flower?" he asked.

"I guess I see the image in the form of a real flower," I said, less sure of myself.

"I'm totally confused," he said. "Let's not talk about it for a while."

He knew what he had done again, twisted my thoughts and explanations to make me seem stupid and then he dropped the entire subject. My mind was going crazy and my thoughts had absolutely no coherence; and all he could say was, "Let's not talk about it for a while."

We began walking again with the old man leading the way. I had not been able to turn my mind off from our previous conversation. He, on the other hand, was totally wrapped up in the beauty of the surroundings and explaining the balance of nature in terms of letting go.

When he noticed that I was not paying attention to what he was saying, he stopped on the trail and said, "Do you ever stop thinking?"

"Yes, sometimes," I said.

"Sometimes my most meaningful realizations come when I don't think," he said. "You're missing the beauty of this walk by thinking so hard. What can be so important?"

"You're right," I said. "It's just a mental game anyway. I know flowers are real."

As we continued to walk, I also became lost in the beauty around me, and periods of time seemed to pass unaccounted for, as if I were day-dreaming.

The old man stopped, turned abruptly, and looked directly at me, as I blurted out, "Do you mean all that I really see are images constructed by my mind?"

"What do you think?" he said.

"I think that's preposterous!" I said. "If I get hit by a speeding truck, that's certainly not a figment of my imagination!" I exclaimed.

"I certainly agree with you there," he said laughing. I never saw him laugh so hard and so long. I stood there feeling foolish, not knowing what the joke was.

"Does that mean that your mind does not create

the image?" he said quizzically.

"Okay, so what if my mind does create the image?" I asked.

"Nothing," he said, "it just seems interesting that your mind creates images in an attempt to *mimic* reality. I was wondering how accurately is it able to reproduce reality?"

"Fairly accurately, I'd say." I could see the old man groping for some smart question to make me look stupid and feel frustrated again.

We started back toward the house in silence. I had finally shut him up. I felt kind of sorry in a way and was hoping he might come up with one of his ingenious questions.

When we reached the front porch, he sat down very heavily. He looked tired, probably more from losing than our excursion.

Then he smiled and asked, "How do you think I feel?"

"Tired," I said.

"Wrong, I feel invigorated. Long walks make my blood flow faster. How far do you think we walked?"

"About 10 miles," I said.

"Wrong. It was exactly 7.5 miles. Look way over yonder in that field. Is Mr. Cooper coming toward us or moving away from us?"

"Looks like he's moving slowly away from us."

"Wrong again," he said, and just about fell off of his chair laughing.

"What's so funny?" I asked when he finally regained control.

"That's Mr. Cooper's scarecrow in the cornfield and he doesn't take walks except on Halloween!"

"Very funny," I said. "What's the point of these foolish questions?"

"Oh, nothing. I was just testing the accuracy of

your mental images," he said with the twinkle and grin.

"Have you ever lost yourself in a flower?" he asked in a very serious tone, looking at me directly.

"Lost myself in a flower?" I asked.

"Yes," he said smiling.

"You mean, appreciated its beauty and form?"

"No! Lost yourself," he said impatiently.

"You mean, periods when I lost track of time while appreciating its beauty?"

"Think carefully," he said, "during those periods, did you lose track of time and appreciate its beauty simultaneously?"

After thinking about his question for a minute or so, I said, "When I lose track of time, everything stops. There is no appreciation or any thinking for that matter. It's when I come back to reality that I say to myself, 'How beautiful the flower is.'"

"During these periods, is there any difference between you and the flower?" he asked in an unattached manner.

"I don't know," I replied. "the question doesn't make sense when asked about such periods."

"Are you saying that the difference between you and the flower exists when you are thinking and your mind is creating mental images?" he asked.

"I'm saying that's the only time the question makes sense to me."

He got up heavily and went inside, returning in five minutes with two lemonades. He handed me one and we both sat there for an hour or so deep within our own private thoughts.

I was, as usual, totally confused.

Chapter 3

If the past is a thought recalled from memory, and the future is a thought about a thought that might happen, and the present is all we have as reality in experience, then, my God, don't touch that and turn "it" into illusion.

When I returned to La Roche two days later, there was no trace of the old man, so I decided to sit on the porch and wait. After I waited for about 45 minutes, deep in thought about how radically my life had changed in just three days as a result of being around this strange old man, he suddenly appeared before me as if he had come from nowhere.

"You said I was welcome to stop by any time, so, I thought I'd drive out and keep you company for a couple of hours."

He just grinned slightly and said, "I was off exploring and lost track of time. You know how limiting it can be living in an old body such as mine."

"Well, at least you have all the time in the world, with nothing to do but live out here. You know, no one knows of this place in New Orleans. It's like it sprang up out of nowhere."

"Really?" he said. "It doesn't matter, because a moment is the same as eternity."

"What do you mean?" I said.

"Exactly what I said, there's no difference between eternity and now!"

"Eternity is endless and timeless," I said suspiciously, "and now will be the past, and what hasn't happened yet is the future."

"You mean like the song *As Time Goes By*?" he asked, amused.

"Yes," I said, "like *As Time Goes By*!"

"Let me see if I understand what you're saying: the past is some number of 'nows' ago, right?"

"Right!" I said.

"How do you know now, what happened several nows ago?"

"That's easy, I simply remember."

"What do you mean by remember?"

"I recall an event from my memory, and describe it in detail. Look old man, I know you're pretty smart and wise, and you like to make me look foolish, but past, present, and future are just like A, B, C. Why do you think we have watches, clocks, oscilloscopes, and all of our sophisticated time measuring devices?"

"I guess you're right; sometimes I get lost in time. I guess my mind is starting to play tricks on me as I get older."

"Don't worry, old man, my grandmother had the same problem when she got old. She often had that far away look and was always asking what time was it."

The old man looked defeated. I guess a moment could seem like an eternity for him, so I thought I'd cheer him up a little by sharing some abstract concepts from physics.

"You know in subatomic physics, the more accurately we know the change in energy of a process, the more ambiguous is our knowledge of the change in time. It's called the Uncertainty Principle," I said with pride. No, a lot of pride. After all, the old man deserved it, given what he put me through over the last three days. "So you see, to some extent the off-hand comment you made is somewhat valid in the subatomic world. If the uncertainty in time change is approximately the same as the time of the event, then that time duration and eternity have little difference in meaning; both are essentially timeless, and time as we know it loses meaning."

"When you recall something from memory, is it like mental imaging?" he asked.

"What are you talking about? Where did that question come from?"

"You said the past was essentially created by recalling some event that happened several nows ago, didn't you?"

"Yes, that's what I said. I thought we had resolved that issue about the real world."

"I'm still a little confused," he said. "Bear with me a little longer. Is mental imaging the same as thinking of past events and then describing your thoughts?"

"Yes, that's close to it."

"Are you saying that the past is a description of thoughts?"

"No, I'm not saying that at all! What I'm saying is that the past is what actually happened previously."

"Is it happening now?" he asked grinning.

"Obviously not," I said, a little irritated at his asking me a stupid question.

"Then, if the past isn't happening now, then it's not reality, is it?"

"No, but it was reality when it happened," I explained excitedly.

"But that *was* a now, wasn't it?" he asked faking a confused look. "And that now *was* the present then, wasn't it?'

"Yes, but it did happen and that's all that counts."

He gave that defeated look again and said wearily, "I guess you're right, from what you said. It just appears to me that now is the only reality there is and the past is our thoughts about reality."

"Okay, suppose I accept that," I said with resignation.

He appeared to be thinking as if he were lost, and then he looked directly at me and said, "Since our thoughts are not reality, perhaps the past (as time) is an illusion, simply made real by agreement."

"I think we are simply playing mental games again," I said, using my standard response whenever I think I have lost. It also provided me an opportunity to buy some time until I could come back with some intelligent counterpoint. "What about the future?"

The old man looked away for about five minutes playing his usual hard-of-hearing game trying to lure me into one of his put-your-foot-in-your-mouth numbers.

So I simply repeated the same question, "What about the future?"

"What about it?" he said.

"It will certainly be moments of now, won't it?"

"Yes."

"Then doesn't that make time real? If the future is real?"

"Well," he said, "if the future hasn't happened, it's a thought from the past about what might happen in the next moment of now. So, it appears to be a thought about a thought," he said with a questioning look. "Isn't it? Help me figure this out."

"If it's a thought about a thought, then it's also an illusion; or more precisely, 'an illusion about an illusion.' But that can't be," I said dejectedly.

"What do you think it all means?" he asked sheepishly.

"I don't know. I can see what you say makes intellectual sense, but I still know there is the past and future. On the other hand, *now* is the only reality I experience."

"I'm not sure any of it makes sense," he said as if the subject was closed and sat back in his chair with that far away look again.

"Look, I'm leaving here at 5:00 p.m. to get back to New Orleans at about 6:15 p.m., and that's no illusion!"

He just sat there as if he didn't even hear me, a voice crying in the wilderness.

After three minutes of my mind doing its usual computer game from being around this old man, I blurted out, "If time is an illusion, it sure makes practical sense to use it!"

He looked at me in a strange way and said softly, "I agree."

On my way back to New Orleans, I noticed some purple wild flowers that must have bloomed recently. The air was totally different from the city, carrying the integrated scents of magnolias, wild flowers, rich soil, and an almost mystical calmness.

As I crossed the city limit, I thought how good it was to be back in reality again.

Chapter 4

University: the study and acceptance of advanced concepts that qualify me to become a practitioner of more advanced illusion.

These advanced illusions are, however, both useful and practical as tools to facilitate my acquisition of wisdom through participation and expanded awareness.

These illusions, in and of themselves, are not the source of wisdom; I am.

What continued to bother me about the conversation I had with the old man was the implication that illusion was a practical part of everyday living. At least that was my extrapolation, and I certainly was no dummy. How many other *possible illusions* were there around that I might be unaware of? This question was most unsettling.

No one ever told me explicitly that the study of science, and physics in particular, was the study of reality. Somehow that seemed to be one of those unquestioned truths about which we all agreed; that had certainly been my assumption. However, that assumption had come under serious scrutiny during my first meeting with the old man. I could slowly begin to feel myself questioning more of the assumptions around me.

The old man had said during one of our conversations, "If you want to discover that which is illusion, concentrate your attention on *what is* or *what actually happens*. Therein, you will discover the rules bounding the game. Once you understand the rules bounding the game, you can then become an effective player. Most, if not all, of the rhetoric about the game by those who think they control the game is a diversion in order to keep you committed to the illusion, as though the game were reality."

As usual, I told him I didn't understand what he was talking about and asked if he had any examples of a so-called game.

He said, "The one you are now playing."

"What game is that?" I asked.

"University."

"University?"

"Yes, University," he said with a disinterested air.

"My attendance at the University is no game," I assured him. "I am preparing myself to be a responsible, functional, and contributing member of society."

"They've taught you well," he said.

I ignored his comment and stuck to the high road. "Tell me what you mean by the game called University."

"Maybe I spoke too quickly," he replied defensively. "Let me see if I understand how the University works. How do you get into a University?" he asked.

"By a stringent selection process in most situations; the best high school students are accepted."

"Of the students who are accepted, how many are still there after the first year?"

"I don't really know. I would guess about 75% at most Universities."

"What happened to the *stringently selected* 25% who are no longer there?"

"They simply couldn't measure up to the requirements."

"Do you think there was ever a group who measured up 95%, or has it been 75% fairly consistently?"

"What's your implication, old man?"

"I was just asking a question about what has actually happened on a consistent basis. I hope that's okay with you."

"Sure, that's okay with me. I just wanted to explain that the high schools where these students come from are very different in terms of their academic preparation for the University. That's why 25% or so never make it past the first year. There are also other complicated factors that create this result on a recurring basis, but I think it'll just confuse the issue to go into them."

"Would you agree then, that one of the rules bounding the game called University is that approximately 25% of the first year group are eliminated?"

"Well, if we are strictly going by *what is*, I guess so."

"How many of the original group actually graduate?" he asked with a disinterested look.

"I don't know exactly. I would guess about 50%," I said, feeling this wasn't a piece of information that was going to work to my advantage.

"Let me see if I understand what actually happens," he said, appearing to gain some interest in the conversation. "Somewhere around 50% is the graduation rate as a bounding rule? Then, no matter what, only 50% of the starting group will graduate?"

"Wait one minute!" I said excitedly. "I have trouble with your use of the word *will*. If more students were adequately prepared then the percentage graduating would probably be higher."

"Well, you told me yourself how much you like the small classes as a junior and looked forward to even more selective ones as a senior, didn't you?"

"Yes, but what does that have to do with the graduating percentage?"

"Well, if the University retained 95%, would they have the resources such as teachers, assistants, money, etc. and facilities such as classrooms, laboratory space, supplies, etc. to accommodate all of these students as juniors and seniors?" he asked in his usual confused way. I knew I was getting into trouble when his eyes started to come alive.

"I guess they might not at present, but they could always get more if required."

"Remember, our bounding rules are based on *what is* and what has apparently consistently happened. Okay?"

"What's the point, old man?" I asked irritably.

"Well," he said slowly, "no matter how hard or not hard 50% of the starting group works, they will not graduate, and this is a bounding rule of the game called University."

"So what?"

"Well, if you were going to play this game, and someone told you a rule is that only 50% graduate no matter what they do, then the way you played the game might be different. It might even influence your decision to play the game at all. Maybe a significant fraction of the 50% might choose not to be part of the *phase-out* process over their University visit."

"I think most students are aware of this situation; if not, they certainly should be."

"Were you when you began?" he asked nonchalantly.

"I never had to worry about that problem, so it was never an issue for me."

He paused for a minute or so apparently on the verge of saying something profound, and from nowhere began to laugh that foolish laugh as if he knew something I didn't.

"Have you read a book titled *Hope for the Flowers*?"

"No, what's it about?"

"Caterpillars."

"Caterpillars? What does that have to do with our discussion?" I asked drawing on my extreme patience. I even crossed my fingers and silently whispered, God, please help me to tolerate this old man.

"Nothing."

"Then why did you bring it up?"

"Because you remind me of Stripe the star caterpillar in the story."

"In what way?"

"He was successful, just as you are; he was very proud of his accomplishments and deservedly so." He took a long breath and sat deeply into his chair with that far away look again. To tell the truth, I kind of liked the old man. What started out as harmless mental gymnastics was starting to have me view the world from a perspective I had never considered before. The most irritating aspect to me was that it started to make more sense from this different perspective.

"What about grading?" he asked in a disinterested manner looking out into the yard.

"What about it?" I replied.

"Have you ever taken a class where everyone made an A?"

"No."

"Have you ever taken a class where most everyone made an A and the remainder B's?"

"No. Look, most or practically all of my classes end up with a final distribution of about 2.75 GPA on a 4.00 system; A's, B's, C's, etc. Is that what you want to know?"

He paused before speaking and finally said, "I don't mean to upset you, perhaps we ought to take a walk."

"That's a good idea. I was getting bored from sitting for so long." I began wondering, as we walked, how he planned to have grades become a bounding rule. After all, what other system would he substitute in place of grading? After we had walked for about a half-mile, I asked, "What's so bad about grades?"

"What?" he said, as though he had come out of a trance.

"What's so bad about grades?" I repeated.

"Nothing."

"Then what's the point you want to make?" I asked again.

"I don't have a point to make. I just wondered about the purpose of grades."

"Grades obviously reflect the level of mastery a student has of a given subject."

"Is there a certain level for earning an A?"

"Of course, there is," I replied impatiently. This old man certainly knew how to get me excited even when I was determined to stay calm. Particularly, when I was determined to stay calm.

"If everyone reached that level, would they all get A's?" he asked easily.

"Obviously not," I replied. "then grades would be meaningless. Anyway, a bounding rule is based on *what is*, remember and what is, is that students perform as a distribution in terms of mastery of any subject. The grades reflect that."

"Then would it be fair to say that no matter how hard students work, the level of mastery is always a distribution as a bounding rule?"

"Yes, I'm comfortable with that statement."

"Then grades are not about fairness or unfairness, as a priority, but about creating the distribution as a bounding rule."

"Not exactly. The distribution is a fair measure of their performance." I waited for his reply, but none came. He just started walking again with his shoulders positioned in such a way to indicate that the discussion was over.

Even though I felt I had won the discussion in explaining how the University truly works, the issues he raised had stimulated a new awareness in me. "To discover that which is illusion, concentrate your attention on *what is* or what actually happens."

Professors practically always give grades of A, B, C, D, F; therefore a bounding rule is that professors must grade as a distribution regardless of class performance. Presumably, they have no choice. So our job as students is to compete for the fixed 10% A's, 30% B's, etc.

It took me several days of thinking and much confusion before it finally hit me over the head. In order to earn A's I have to literally think as they do, therefore I'm a clone or something sufficiently close so that there is no essential difference; and that's a bounding rule. But most of all, I am certified to continue practicing the only true reality there is. And if I want to be a guiding light in determining the extension of the only true reality, I must be exposed to more of the same until I completely lose touch with "it might be another way." Now I'm ready to be a practitioner.

Somehow, I wanted all of this to be wrong. I wanted someone to show me that my reasoning was faulty somewhere; or better still, totally. The old man was the last person I wanted to see. So I hung out in my University world for a week or so hoping that my crazy thoughts about *bounding rules* would fade away into the sunset. I guess the problem I had was that my conclusions about the game called University were realizations and not intellectual classroom discussions.

Chapter 5

If we are all intrinsically worthy by virtue of being created, then how did illusions such as self-worth and self-esteem ever creep into our language as realities?

The problem is, there is no one to talk to when these things happen. And what I want to do most of all is to tell someone of the marvelous discovery I made, primarily because it's so freeing.

I mentioned the possibility to some of my fellow students who were particularly open-minded that free and original expression at the University was an illusion, especially where students were concerned. First, I got everyone's undivided attention, then dead silence, and finally, stares of disbelief.

After a short recovery period, they were quick to point out how ours was one of the leading Universities in the country in the Arts, Sciences, and Medicine. I was reminded of the series of articles published last year by one of our leading sociologists about the treatment of minorities at the University and the coverage it got nationwide. The president of the University was both outraged and embarrassed. The sociologist stood his ground and went on to suggest that the key to significant change in the performance of minorities was dependent on their sense of self-worth or self-esteem; and that the University had a responsibility to devise programs to increase both. If that wasn't an example of free expression, then what was I looking for? (They went on to cite at least five more examples of original work in several disciplines, much to my dismay at being unable to back up my assertion.)

Somehow, somewhere in all of this, I knew what I was talking about, but being able to defend it logically in a language we all understood was something else. I wished I had the old man there with me to put them through the same kind of exercise he put me through. Or maybe I could say, I know this old man who lives forty miles northwest of New Orleans, in a one-house town forgotten by time, who could clear all this up with a few well-designed questions. However, things were bad enough. The next time I blurt out something like that again, I thought, I'll be ready.

When I finished relating the story to the old man the next day, I told him how stupid and deflated I felt. He just sat there offering no sympathy or suggested arguments. In fact, he really looked disinterested, if the truth be told. "Just like the minorities, huh?"

"What?"

"You lost your self-esteem?" he said understandingly.

"Yes, somewhat; but nothing that can't be recovered."

"What about your self-worth?"

"What about it?"

"Did you lose it, too?"

"No, my self-worth was just fine. Why are you asking me these questions? I'm more interested in your helping me to understand why academic freedom at the University is an illusion."

"How much did you lose?" he asked.

"How much of what?"

"Your self-esteem?"

"I don't know. It doesn't come in amounts like pounds or bushels, you know."

"Well, how does it come? You agreed that you *somewhat* lost your self-esteem and your self-worth."

"Wait a minute, my self-worth is just fine. It's the minorities who have lowered self-worth. At least that's what our leading sociologist thinks."

"Do you agree?"

"Yes, I think they would do better if they had a greater sense of self-worth. I know that both play an important role in my performance."

"How high?"

"How high what?"

"How high should their lowered self-worth be raised? The minorities."

"I don't know exactly, I just said it can't be measured."

"How do you know yours is high?"

"I just tell myself and know I mean it."

"Why can't they just tell themselves and mean it also?"

"I don't know, why don't you ask them?"

"Okay, let me see if I understand what you have said. Self-esteem and self-worth go up and down, can't be measured quantitatively, and you know when you do or don't have it. Right?"

"Right."

"I'm confused, how can a person's worth go up and down?" he asked.

"Not their intrinsic worth, only what they think of their worth. That's what's meant by self-worth."

"So, are they intrinsically worthy?"

"Of course, everyone is."

"Then why do we need the term self-worth?"

"Because some people think they're not," I said.

"Suppose we simply treated them as though they were fully worthy? What would happen then? It seems to me if we pretend they don't have self-worth then we keep the illusion in place. Help me here, you understand these things about students, I don't."

"The important point here is that we have to convince them somehow that they are fully worthy. That's what the sociologist was suggesting."

"So in the meantime we pretend they are not and create programs to achieve an illusion? We begin with the illusion they are not fully worthy and proceed to the illusion that their worth has been significantly increased?"

"Look, old man, this isn't my problem. I don't know what they should do. I came here to have you help explain what I realized about the true purpose of the University."

"Why?"

"So I can show my friends I know what I'm talking about."

"You mean regain their respect or win the argument?"

"Both. If I win the argument, I also regain their respect."

"If you regain their respect, will your somewhat lowered self-esteem go up again, also?"

Why did I have this feeling of the rug moving under me and the old man tugging? "Yes," I ventured.

"Then it seems to me that winning is more about ego than self-esteem or self-worth. Particularly for someone like you who now knows he is intrinsically worthy."

"That makes sense, but what's so bad about a strong ego?"

"Nothing. As long as there is the awareness that self-worth and self-esteem are both illusions and what really goes up and down is the ego, in the guise of the more acceptable term self-confidence."

"I have no idea in the world how you conclude that."

"I took a quantum jump; one of my convenient assertions which are allowed with age," he said with the twinkle and the grin. "The important question is why do we keep the illusions of self-worth and self-esteem around (and even put them in the dictionary) as if they are real?"

Chapter 6

Whenever we expose an illusion, we experience a realization, which results in expanded awareness as wisdom and recovered self-responsibility. From self-responsibility, possibilities are infinite!

I could certainly see now that self-esteem and self-worth were both questionable as realities, but even so they seemed to serve some useful purpose. After all, there are millions of books, tapes, seminars, workshops, and classes about improving or increasing self-esteem and self-worth. Why in the world would we spend so much time and money improving or increasing illusion? I even wonder when the expressions came into existence. Jesus of Nazareth, from written accounts, treated everyone as intrinsicly worthy, having no degrees of high, low, or medium, or the necessity of earning worth. I would guess the question of self-worth never came up for an individual to consider when around him. Maybe it's because he never assumed his own worth was greater than any other individual. This whole thing was confusing to me and the old man was of no help at all after initiating this entire process.

When I asked him questions concerning self-esteem and self-worth, he simply smiled and said, "We have the illusions of Santa Claus and the Tooth Fairy, don't we? Why not self-esteem and self-worth?" and then fell over laughing again saying, "You'll figure it out. Remember, confusion is a great place to be. It means movement from limited awareness to expanded awareness; that process is always accompanied by confusion."

The old man said, "Whenever you are confused, concentrate on what is, in order to discover the bounding rules of the game or the illusion." I was determined to figure this one out for myself, no matter how long it might take. Given what the old man said, I'm not sure he was willing to help me anyway. "Hang out with your confusion, rub it all over you, and most of all, don't pretend you're not confused or resist it; that only prolongs the process and makes you physically uncomfortable. After all, the real battle is with your ego, which assumes it should know and make sense of everything according to how it's *already* put together."

If I assume that both self-esteem and self-worth are realities, then it immediately creates a system for distinguishing between and among people. It also provides a measure for those distinctions, albeit nebulous, that everyone believes to be true. That is, some people are high in esteem or worth and some are low in the first place. What we have then is a system in place for the legitimate creation of some people being "better than" and some "less than" by necessity of creating "better than." One brings the other into existence, much the same as "yes" creates "no," "good" creates "evil," "wrong" creates "right." This is the wonderful world of dichotomies that I learned in Philosophy 101. The instant I create a value, I simultaneously create its opposite, and both become part of my system for judging and evaluating other people and myself.

Superimposing our value system of symbols of success, then high self-esteem and self-worth are in general, but not always, synonymous with a successful and correspondingly superior individual and low self-esteem and self-worth are in general, but not always, synonymous with an unsuccessful and correspondingly inferior individual. In simple language, it appears to me that esteem and worth are somehow connected to symbols of achievement and success. So, if I have stumbled through this process with any degree of sanity at all, one of the bounding rules of these illusions is to keep in place the superior-inferior distinctions between people.

I don't know if I like this process; the truth is, I don't like this process because I can feel myself becoming uncomfortable. It's almost like accusing myself of being superior to other people. The truth is, I do think I am superior to some people, but that's because I've proven it by my accomplishments, by my symbols of success, or more recently, by how I've expanded my awareness beyond my immediate reality. I can't believe I'm really saying all these things. I should have left that old man to get his own ride the first day we met, then I wouldn't be in this state of confusion saying things to myself that I can't distinguish as truth or non-truth anymore.

I walked out into my yard and felt the warm sun pour over, around, and into my entire body. The flow of energy seemed to be particularly strong from the top of my head, down through my spine, and then it spread throughout my entire body. Somehow, I felt good from a place inside of me I couldn't understand, even though I was making discoveries about myself I certainly wouldn't want others to know. The funny thing is, I don't know if I would be more upset by them discovering these prejudices that were probably true of me *or* the exposure and collapse of my justified game of superiority.

Therefore, pretending these illusions or thought-realities to be real paradoxically keeps the first bounding rule in place. That is, the inferior individual can never quite acquire as much self-esteem or self-worth as the individual desperately attempting to bring him up to a higher level. It's as though the more his esteem or worth increases, the higher he has to go. This is a common characteristic of illusions, they are unquantifiable and ultimately unattainable. After all, how can one achieve an illusion? Even the individual who claims to be superior will admit that he, too, is not fully esteemed or totally worthy. I guess the second bounding rule of this game is that full self-esteem or self-worth is not attainable. Another way of stating this bounding rule is that we can't create reality from illusion. What we have created is a game without end, unless of course, we expose the illusion and our individual investments in keeping the illusion in place.

Somehow, I don't like the feeling in my stomach that immediately arises with the previous thought. After all, I don't live my life thinking about esteem or worth; if someone has a problem in that area that's his affair and I assume it has little or nothing to do with me. Then why is my stomach doing what it is doing? Damn that old man. It's all his fault. I can see him probably laughing, while I'm here squirming. I was feeling proud of myself, in that, I didn't need the old man to probe and push, which always gave me my excuse to protest and resist his assertions.

Let's see, what's the question again? What are our individual investments in keeping the illusions in place? My personal answer is "none." Except there goes my stomach again. I guess I did say that I do feel superior to some people and that my own sense of self-esteem and self-worth were significant factors, particularly where achievement is concerned. Since this is a private conversation, I guess I can at least admit to myself that I do have an investment in these illusions being real.

Well, in academic competition, if I can gain an edge over other students (majority or minority) because they believe they have low self-esteem or low self-worth, that's just fine with me. I would probably be willing to have a long conversation with them about how they might work to improve both. Probably, as long as I discussed the situation as if it were real, they would be less of a threat to my excelling. I can't believe I'm saying this, but my stomach is in complete agreement. I wonder if I also use this game or something similar to it outside of academics. That is, keep people disabled by sympathizing with their lack of ability to withstand the "slings and arrows" of the world. I probably have, but I didn't know then what I was doing. Why can't I just tell my mind to slow down or better still, just stop? This process is obviously going too far too fast.

It's like going down a smooth tube with nothing to grab and asking myself, how did I get here? Surely I didn't consciously put myself into this situation.

But, what do *they* have to gain? What possible investment could an individual have in being low in esteem or worth? There's that voice again, "Concentrate on what happens."

Let's see, I guess in general, they're not expected to perform at the same level as someone who is high in esteem or worth. They aren't as accountable for what happens, because everyone understands their difficulty. Therefore, what happens is that someone low in self-esteem or self-worth does not have to claim responsibility for the results he produces. That appears to be a bounding rule. If all of a sudden that individual did claim responsibility, he or she would discover instantaneously the illusion, and his or her life would transform. That is, they would experience an irreversible positive change in living. It seems everywhere I turn or whenever I get to the bottom of any significant issue, self-responsibility is also always waiting there.

Chapter 7

More often than not, man operates under the illusion that there is choice. There is no choice, only the way it is; and the way it is, is singular. What we do have, however, is the freedom to "create" every moment of each of our unique paths.

I couldn't contain myself, I was so eager to tell the old man what I discovered on my own. Mostly, that I didn't need his help to figure out the illusions of self-esteem and self-worth and the implications of keeping them in place. Oops! There goes my ego again. Most of all, I liked the feeling of being freed from the necessity of carrying around that *superiority mantle*. I had not been conscious of the energy, time, and effort I unconsciously devoted to keeping it in place.

When I allowed myself permission to really look, what I discovered (as I previously pointed out) was that my esteem and worth were synonymous with my personal achievements. Therefore, if I achieved distinction relative to my peers, my esteem and worth were high, but not as high as possible though, because an illusion is infinite. If I were not achieving distinction, then they were low. This insight allowed me to uncouple human worthiness from human achievement as a bounding rule for my life.

When I excitedly shared this with the old man, he did his usual number, nothing. But I did notice an almost imperceptible expression in his eyes of genuine joy. Then he sat back abruptly and said, "Just like Stripe."

"What?"

"Just like Stripe," he repeated.

"Who's Stripe?"

"You know, the caterpillar we were discussing the other day."

"You mean the one who was so proud of his accomplishments?"

"Yes."

"What does that have to do with me?"

"He discovered there was nothing at the top, except more of the same and that it took more energy, time, and effort to remain there. But at least he discovered it."

"What did he do then?"

"He simply climbed back down to a level where all the caterpillars were equal, one and the same."

I nodded as though I understood, but I didn't. Something strange happened for the first time. I noticed that I didn't have to struggle with the fact that I didn't understand something fully. Maybe if I just opened myself up to be receptive to what he was saying, it would come to me later. So I did. It felt good not to be reacting as much to the old man. I think I caught a glimpse again of that genuine joy in his eyes. "You mean he sat on a rock and contemplated life?"

The old man roared with laughter until tears were rolling from his eyes. I had never seen him laugh so hard. I didn't realize what I had said was so funny. We often made comments like that about our university professors.

"In essence, yes, for the first time in his life; and then he did what he wanted to."

Since the old man continued to laugh, so did I. I felt foolish if I didn't join in. And yet I felt foolish laughing since I didn't really know the joke. So what, I said to myself, it feels good to laugh, particularly when you don't know what you're laughing about.

"Generally, it takes a long time to find the path when it hasn't as yet been forged," he said.

"How can you find a path that hasn't been forged? That doesn't make any sense."

"I know," he said with his usual impatience of tolerating my ignorance. "that's why it's original."

"Okay," I said, using my recently adopted strategy of 'accept it now and understand it later.' "But how do you know when you've found the right path?"

"There are no right or wrong paths; only each individual's unique path that he creates each moment of living. Sometimes it crosses the paths of others and generates conflict for long periods of time. Simply being keenly aware of that path which generates conflict allows one to create spontaneously the path which generates harmony. And that's the path we really want to forge, without prior knowledge."

The old man was getting further and further away from reality or any reality I understood, so I decided to drop my newly found strategy and admitted I had no idea in heaven what he had been talking about for the past five minutes.

He just twinkled and smiled and said, "Accept it now and understand it later."

I have no idea how he figured out my strategy, so I decided to take the high road again; that is, ignore his comment and go on as if I understood. "Is there an alternative way of saying the same thing?" I asked intellectually.

"Yes, as a matter of fact there *is* a much simpler way of saying the same thing: It's an illusion to think it could be any way other than the way it is; and living as if an illusion is real always generates conflict. Does that simplify matters any?"

"Well, it certainly is a concise way of putting it. I have to think on it. Perhaps an example would help."

"Okay, I'm going to ask you to project yourself twenty years or so into the future. This shouldn't be too difficult since you've lived this exercise previously. You've worked painstakingly up the organizational and social ladder to prominence and success, but you can't quite say you've made it. At last you have an opportunity to be President and Chief Executive Officer of your organization. This would finally be *the* step that would have everyone know that you had made it. You have impeccable credentials, no family problems, that is, a well-behaved wife and no kids on alcohol or drugs that you know of, and a dog that selectively bites people of lower caste, and subordinates who are fully supportive of your ascendency to the throne. Finally the day comes for the announcement and you are not chosen. Now really project yourself into this situation in order to make the example effective. Would you be upset?"

"Yes, I think I would be upset," I replied somewhat disappointed about the conclusion of the story.

"No, would you be angry?"

"Probably, it depends on who got the position."

"Who cares, you didn't get it, even though you probably deserved it. Now, how angry would you be?" He was pushing me.

"Very angry!"

"What do you plan to do about it?" he asked sharply.

"Nothing! at least at first." I could feel my blood flowing faster.

"You mean, you're going to stay in that Peter position indefinitely?"

"No! I could probably quit." I could feel myself getting really worked up at this point. Somehow the old man had struck a chord in me that I had no trouble at all living through.

"If you quit, what will you do?" he asked sharply.

"I don't know, I would have to think about it."

"Think about what?" he pushed.

"My life. And what to do about it!" I said angrily.

Then he instantly transformed his expression to the twinkle and the smile and asked, "You mean, you're going to sit on a rock and contemplate life?"

I didn't say anything for about three minutes, at which point he looked at me and said, "Welcome to the top. You just did exactly what was expected according to the bounding rules—quit."

"What's the point of this exercise?" I asked, very irritated.

"I don't know, what do you think?" he asked, as if he were confused along with me.

That's another strategy I had learned from the old man: when you get your opponent on the ropes, knock him out, or when a student is at the height of confusion, answer a question with a more confusing question, and watch his eyes go like a Las Vegas slot machine; and then out drops the realization and exposure of the illusion.

"Well, after discovering what it is really like at the top, I guess I decided I didn't want to play that game anymore."

"Sounds to me like you're a sore loser who didn't pay close enough attention to the rules of the game or maybe at a deeper level you didn't really think the rules applied to you."

"Since I was disappointed and angry, I guess I

really didn't believe the rules applied to me; so in essence, I was living in an illusion, even though I intellectually knew the rules."

"What else did you discover?"

"When my illusion was non-intellectually revealed, I had to make a decision."

"You mean create a crisis," he said easily.

"Are you suggesting that *I* had something to do with their decision not to promote me?"

"Yes, everything."

"That's ludicrous!"

"I know."

"That's like saying I set the entire scheme in motion in order to create a crisis."

"That's a bounding rule, when people decide unconsciously to find the path," he said with the twinkle and the grin. "It's all part of the game."

"That's even more ludicrous!"

"I know. I just simple-mindedly concentrate on what happens and equally simple-mindedly assume that's what was truly intended. Simply because that's what happened. Simple, isn't it?"

I was speechless and said to myself, control son, control. After five minutes or so of my mind doing pirouettes and tailspins, I finally asked, even though something told me I didn't want to know, "What does a crisis have to do with finding the path?"

He thought for a long time and finally looked directly at me and said, "A crisis is a legitimate excuse or acceptable reason for 'sitting on a rock and contemplating your life.' Do you *see* that?"

"Yes, somewhat, but I'm having a difficult time."

"Finding the path is the same as finding yourself, and what you want to do follows spontaneously and naturally, literally without thought or effort.

It's as if there never was anything else to do, and living up to that point had been an illusion. Do you *see* that?" he asked again, somewhat impatiently.

"Yeah, I think I do, but it's not very clear in my mind."

"Listen very closely," he said. "You either do what you do, moment by moment of living, as programmed by your ego in normal fashion or you transcend your ego and do that which is spontaneous and natural. In either case, there is no thought, before the fact, and therefore choice is an illusion."

Chapter 8

If I create my reality, born from my thoughts of what I observe through what I believe, then who I am is my thoughts about reality. What "appears" to me as "out-there" is really "in-here," and the observed and observer are one and the same.

CHAPTER 8

It would be an understatement to say I was confused for the next four days. Whatever strategy I had designed for myself in dealing with the old man had been of absolutely no use.

If what he had said was true, then up to the crisis we discussed, living in an illusion was not only like being in fantasyland, but *I* also created my fantasyland or reality. Or for that matter, we all individually create our realities or our illusions of reality and proceed to live in them as though they are real, until something or someone comes along to burst the bubble; which is the same as a crisis. But what was even more off the wall was the suggestion that *we* also set in motion the events leading to the bursting of our own bubbles! Now that's about the limit that an openminded person could accept. However, he didn't even stop at the limit, but went on to imply that bursting the bubble allows the illusion to be exposed and realized, or as he philosophically put it,

> *Discovering how it is,*
> *is exactly the same as*
> *discovering how it is not.*

These conclusions really began to trouble me because I suspected that more was involved here than was apparent. And if I continued to slide down this chute with the smooth sides with nothing to grab, then I would have no control over where I might end up. I suspected the troubling aspect of the entire situation was that I was already sliding down the chute and had passed the point of no return.

If I create my own reality, it's like having my own Disneyland. Then, what we call reality is what we create from our literally infinite capacity to think. Therefore, we assume our thoughts to be reality and proceed to live within them as if they were the truth.

But wait a minute, other people have the same thoughts as I do about reality; there must be some validity to mass agreement.

Somehow I got the feeling this entire process was proceeding too fast. So I turned on the TV in order to allow my mind to rest and think of something else. That was the worst thing I could do because the instant I let down my conscious resistance to this process, an entire array of uncomfortable thoughts spontaneously erupted. They were accompanied by elation and fear and a sense of exciting discovery.

Then I interpret the "out-there" world through the eyes of my reality. Psychologists have known this for years, that we filter external events through our reality. But this filtration process implies that, that which gets through *is* reality. If my entire reality (for interpretation) is Disneyland, then there is no such thing as filtering parts of the truth. The entire interpretation is a fabrication of my mind and therefore illusion!

Let me back up a minute here. This is the problem with sliding down a chute: It simply bypasses logic or common sense. It simply jumps to conclusions in a discontinuous way, leaving for later, filling in the gaps. The old man once said, "Filling in the gaps with logic is a process that man uses to connect to the base of what he already knows as illusion, and is ultimately meaningless *and* enjoyable." My strategy was "file it now and *maybe* something will come along to resurrect it later. But I hope not."

This process seems to raise questions about terms such as open-mindedness and objectivity. Namely, that there are no such situations as open-mindedness and objectivity. At least, not in the way we use the terms. Everything is as *my* mind interprets it. But why are these words in the dictionary? Is the dictionary in on the conspiracy also? Who wrote the dictionary? I guess we did. Then, this whole thing seems to be a closed circle of illusion, with me in the center of confusion.

When I say I am being objective, I am really expressing my subjective opinion. I guess even the laws of physics, which are considered to be objective knowledge, are an agreed upon collection of subjective opinions based upon our ability to *mimic* natural phenomena rather than knowing the truth about natural phenomena. Objectivity and open-mindedness are both illusions we create through mass agreement—much as most of the world believed the planet to be flat during Columbus' time. And that Earth was the center of the universe, and fixed, or not moving in space, during the time of Copernicus. It is even more interesting, that during that time when Galileo continued the work of Copernicus, his fellow scientists even refused to look through his telescope where they could see for themselves the movement of planetary bodies around the sun. I guess things haven't really changed very much since then.

My velocity down the chute was increasing; I could feel it. If I had come this far, I had essentially lost contact with whatever I was desperately holding on to. So why not just let go totally and see what happens? I did, and just went along for the ride, without resistance or confusion. It was a bit scary because it seemed so natural. If letting go was being natural, then what was the resistance?

When I let go, the next conclusion I came to without logic was, "If I observe the 'out there' world through *my* eyes, then in large part, if not totally, I am observing myself; and the observed and observer are the same." But this is what J. Krishnamurti had spent much of his life expressing to the world—and probably many more had before him. I guess there is really nothing new under the heavens, only realizations in passing.

Now I think I understand what is meant by expressions such as "other people serve as mirrors for us" or "behavior or characteristics we observe about others that we admire or dislike are also true about us."

Finally, I see his point about the path. The path to discovering reality is the realization of one's self. Actually Socrates said it succinctly many centuries ago, "Know thyself," and Shakespeare wrote, "To thine own self be true."

Chapter 9

Oneness is the realization of the illusion of the individual. It is the recognition that harmony in living results from the absence of "I-ness" and "me-ness."

Somehow, I guess discovering reality, if such is possible, begins with the true realization of "in-here." And the quest is not so much the discovery of reality as much as it is the realization of that which is illusion. I can't believe how philosophical I have become. How can one person with an array of simple-minded questions so shake the foundation of my world in three rapid-fire weeks? If I were to ask him, he would probably imply that somehow I *wanted* all of this to happen.

The thing that confuses me most is how I could change so rapidly in such a short period of time. The kinds of things I am saying and thinking should require years of study or visiting Eastern countries and finding masters or sitting on a mountain top until the revelation hits me. All I had was this shabby old man who seemed to be asleep most of the time. This is certainly not the form in which I would expect enlightenment to come.

When I arrived at La Roche several days later, I said to him, "You know my life over the past three weeks has been nothing but a series of cycles involving confusion and realization."

"So what's new?" he replied.

"What's new? That's new. At least for me."

"Not really. It's only been at longer intervals of time before."

"Most of the thoughts I am having, I really don't

know how to integrate into my life. I guess I'm scared."

"Were you scared when you ventured to walk for the first time as a baby?"

"Yes."

"So, what's the difference?"

"But I didn't have a choice about that!"

He looked directly at me for a long thirty seconds and just grinned. I, of course, didn't ask what that meant. Somehow I knew, considering our previous discussions.

"Another thing I can't quite understand," I said, "is why have your questions had such an impact on me? I've had endless philosophical discussions before about God, the meaning of life, who am I, and all the rest with teachers and friends, and those discussions were as quickly forgotten as morning dew by noon. I think I've learned more about myself and life in the past three weeks than most of my years of being educated in school."

"Maybe that's a bounding rule," he said with a disinterested look.

"But, I always thought," and I stopped in mid-sentence knowing what he was thinking by the long stare he gave me. Sometimes it felt as though the old man could actually plant thoughts in my head. I had concluded some time ago that he read my thoughts, especially those I wanted to hide most. But now we had this system of communication which didn't require seeing or hearing or any of the other senses, for that matter.

"What do *you* think is the difference?" he asked.

"Well, you certainly aren't as smart or intelligent as my professors. No offense old man, but my teachers do have Ph.D.'s and years of studying almost every book on their subject of interest." Actually, I enjoyed that comment and looked out of the corner of my eye for his reaction.

He simply grinned, scratched his head, and said easily, "I guess you're right about that. What do you think is the difference?"

"I don't think I really know for sure. Either what you asked or the way you asked, somehow touched a place in me that was not so easy to reject outright, as were my intellectual discussions."

"Anything else?"

"Yeah, I never felt any sense of competition from you. As if you didn't really have any investment in winning or losing a point."

The old man looked up quickly and said, "We've stumbled upon another illusion."

"What illusion is that?"

"The one you just mentioned," he replied.

"I didn't mention any illusion; I just said I never felt any competition about winning and losing."

"That's it."

"That's what?"

"The illusion."

"You mean winning and losing?"

"Yes," he said as though I had reached the gateway to the bank.

"Yeah, I know, it's how you play the game. Let's come back to that subject later."

"Okay, anything else?"

"No books! We didn't use a single book! I learned all I learned without the use of one book *and* you didn't really give me any answers. Only frustration."

"Why do you think it was so frustrating not to have answers from me?"

"Because, whenever I've had a problem or a situation in life there has always been someone there to give or suggest to me the answer. So, at first it was difficult to adjust to this way of relating."

"What did you discover?"

"If I was willing to be frustrated and confused then I could work out things for myself. Funny thing, the solutions that other people suggested to me ultimately never worked. I wonder why?"

"What do you think?"

I thought about his question for several minutes and up popped an insight. "I think, at a deeply unconscious level, I probably had no intention of their solutions working; most likely because their solutions to my problems were the best solutions for their problems. I guess the best solutions or answers ultimately come from inside of me, whether I am aware I am using my own solutions or not."

"Do you think that source has any limit?"

"I don't know. I'm only beginning to understand what's been happening to me over the past three weeks. So far, every time I searched, I got something, not always what I was looking for. I'll just keep using that source until it proves to be empty."

He smiled and said, "Who knows, it may just be infinite."

I took the high road again and changed the subject. "What about winning and losing?" I asked, attempting to get him on the defensive for once.

"Maya," he said.

"Maya? What's maya?"

"A Sanskrit word meaning illusion."

"I think we're going a little *too* far now. Most of television sports, programs, and just about everything in life is based upon competition and winning and losing. Haven't you ever heard of the 'agony of defeat?' "

"So what?" he said, "Billions of dollars are

based on Santa Claus and the Easter Bunny. As long as people believe an illusion is so, then it's so. Even if it isn't so." Then he began laughing again as if he had scored points on me; that somehow I was an eager participant in a global charade and why didn't I have the intelligence to see it.

"Why would the media promote such illusion, *if* what you say has any validity at all?"

"They simply provide what we want. They have no choice in the matter either; that's a bounding rule. Okay, let me try it a different way. What does it mean to you to win and how do you feel when you've won something?'

"I guess it's a demonstration of a greater level of mastery and superiority in some activity. I feel better when I win than when I lose."

"What do you mean by feel better?" he asked.

"Well, better than the person who lost."

"Do you identify with his losing?'

"No, I guess I don't. I feel better than him."

"So here we are again making distinctions, only this time we seem to have stumbled upon a universal way that totally permeates the planet."

"Are you telling me that you don't enjoy competing or observing competitive activities, old man?"

"No, I enjoy them immensely," he said easily.

"Then, what's the point?" I said, confused.

"There is no point, just the observation. In fact, I agree with just about everything you've said."

"Then what do you disagree with?" I asked, annoyed.

He paused for a long time as if thinking over a very complex question.

"What do you disagree with?" I asked again.

"The separateness," he said.

"What separateness?"

"The *feeling* that you are a winner and he is a loser; that appears to be separateness to me. What do you think?" he asked.

"Well, if I truly identified with his loss, then my winning would be meaningless."

He went into his wide grin and said, "We're back at maya."

"I don't accept that," I said.

"I didn't think you would. Do you think you *could* identify with his loss if you wanted to?"

"I don't know, I never tried to, but I guess I could if I really wanted to."

"Would you say that, so far, you have not unconsciously wanted to?"

"I guess so," I replied cautiously.

"Are you afraid of what might happen if you tried it once?"

"I guess so."

"What do you think might happen?" he asked seriously.

"Well, if I discovered winning and losing to be an illusion in a tennis game, then it would probably be an illusion in school, in business, on TV, and who knows where it might stop!"

"Suppose it didn't stop?" he asked with greater seriousness.

"Then *I* would simply stop thinking about it and forget the entire subject. For that matter, the subject of this entire discussion we're having could be an illusion."

"It is," he said, and sat back in his chair in his usual way of indicating the discussion was over. That is, I could continue to ask questions, but he would close his eyes and pretend to be asleep.

Here I was again, at my usual place, confused. Given where I was, there was nothing to ask anyway. After what appeared to be fifteen minutes of my mind doing roller derby, he asked, "How do you feel when you hear of an airplane crash and people killed?"

"I feel bad," I said rather indignantly at such an obvious question.

"Why do you think you feel bad?"

"Because I think my family or friends could have been killed in such a horrible way."

"What about you?"

"Yes, I think of myself, too. In fact, it feels most uncomfortable when I think about me."

"When you first hear or read about such an incident, do you think of yourself, family, and friends first, and then feel bad?"

"No, I immediately feel bad."

"Even without knowing who they are?" he asked.

"Yes, even without knowing who they are," I said, wanting him to know that I was a sensitive human being.

"What do you think is the reason for the way you feel about friends and family?"

"That's simple, I know them. I have a relationship with them."

"What about people you don't know? You said you feel bad about them also, didn't you?"

"I don't know. I guess I could possibly relate to their tragedy also."

"Does that mean you have a relationship with them also? Even though you don't know them personally?"

"I guess so, in a remote way."

"Would you feel differently if the people were Russian?"

I started to blurt out, I feel equally about all people where the value of human life is concerned, but underneath it all, I knew I would feel less concerned if they were Russians. Even so, I felt a sense of concern at a level that was impossible to express to others and difficult to admit to myself.

My mind immediately drifted back to a French exchange student who studied at the University for a year. I certainly was as close to her as any American friend I had. Even the recent relationship I had with a Chinese student was of the same intensity as my family. Then there was my friend from Czechoslovakia whom I had come to love but would never tell him.

I guess I never really thought about relationships with people from other countries. How did they differ from the Russians? The truth is, I never met a Russian. All I know about Russians is what I've read, been told, or seen on TV, which has always been consistent with what I've read and been told. Somehow, I was getting this uneasy feeling again of the circle of illusion and me at the center of confusion.

"I guess, you could say that I'm *remotely* related to Russians, but I totally disagree with what they believe."

"So, if you put beliefs aside for the moment, all you have is relationship," he said smiling.

"I can't do that," I said flatly. "I don't trust them."

"I understand," he said with a look that seemed to say, "I guess that's the way it is."

We both just sat with our thoughts as the cool late afternoon breeze seemed to be a glue or a medium that connected me and the old man in some way that was beyond my comprehension.

I looked up, somehow sensing he was about to ask a question. There's that communication again.

"What if we, as human beings, derived meaning *from* relationship?"

"I don't understand what you mean?'

"Instead of viewing a relationship from the perspective that you and I, as separate entities, give meaning or definition to our relationship, suppose our relationship always existed and gave meaning to us?"

"That doesn't make sense at all!"

He looked annoyed at me for the first time and said, "Don't you ever use your mind to do anything except think in circles?"

"Well, the things you ask are not everyday Sunday afternoon party questions, you know."

"I know that. Why do you think I chose you?"

"Chose me for what?"

"Chose you to provide me with entertainment," he said shifting from his serious look to his familiar grin.

"Let me see, if I pictured a relationship as the glue that holds us together, much like the electron density between two atoms forms a chemical bond, then the center of importance is the glue or the bond, and you and I are not so important as separate entities."

"Keep going," he encouraged, as he noticed I was in the chute again.

"Then, in some way, I don't quite understand as yet, *me* as a separate entity from *you* is an illusion! But that can't be," I quickly added.

He looked at me with that look that said, "You're already out of the other end of the chute." Then he said aloud, "You know a bounding rule of the chute is conclusions or quantum jumps without meaning. Filling in the details is just intellectual mumbo jumbo that any idiot can do."

"Is that a reference to me?"

"Obviously no, why do you ask such a silly question?"

I took the high road again. It suddenly appeared to me that I had been using the high road a lot lately.

"*If* you and I as separate entities is an illusion, then why doesn't the same rule apply to everyone I know; or even individuals I don't know?" I asked.

"I think you're carrying this too far," the old man said less serious and more mocking.

"No, I'm not; it's a logical extension."

"I think you're really going too far," he said again.

"If we're *all* related and *indistinguishable* from one another, then we're simply one."

"One what?" he asked with his silly grin.

"One, just one."

I looked at him with the excited sense of a baby discovering his fingers and toes. He just sat back in his chair, took a long deep sigh as if *he* had worked through a very difficult situation, and he closed his eyes.

My mind was into all-out rebellion; red alert was flashing throughout my head. Rockets and fireworks were going off, and he just sat there with his eyes closed.

Something had snapped inside of me, not physically, of course. But something had definitely happened. I was so scared, I don't know if I even liked it or not. The only thought I had was, something happened and I would never be the same again.

CHAPTER 9

When I became conscious again, after a period of time I had no comprehension of, he was asking me a question. It sounded as though he was far off in some other land, or maybe I was. In any case, I finally said, "What?"

"Can you come by tomorrow about 8:30 a.m., I think we're all finished."

"Sure." I certainly agreed with him about being finished. I had had quite enough for one day. When I got up to leave, I had a difficult time keeping my balance at first. It was as if my foundation had been shaken.

Chapter 10

If it's all an illusion, everything that is, and I can still learn, grow, and gain wisdom in terms of bringing harmony and love to the planet by pretending everything is real, though "knowing" it's not, then what difference does it really make?

"I don't have a problem," I said, looking deeply into the old man's eyes for the first time. It seemed as though the depths were infinite, beyond feeling and sensing to an inner calm of knowing with sureness; wisdom.

Much of what he had taught me began to make sense as I started to notice more around me from day to day, such as living more in the moment and allowing for more spontaneity. In such situations, I found myself losing track of significant gaps of time and during those periods of losing myself, time in a practical sense, was an illusion.

I must admit, I have also begun to look at my study of physics quite differently. I am more aware that I set-up, tamper with, and predispose every experiment I perform. I am at least convinced that the study of the physical laws as practiced does include me and that our theories contain that character, flavor, and prejudice.

"I'll be leaving soon," he said quietly.

"What? Why? Where will you go?"

"I'm all finished here. There's nothing more to do. I'm going back to where I came from. I need to be reunited with friends and loved ones."

"I can certainly understand that, old man. Family is in the final analysis, all we really have of each other. When do you plan to return?" I asked.

"Oh, by and by. I guess mostly when I'm needed."

Here he goes again, I said to myself, but I wasn't going to get suckered this time. So I simply replied, "I know what you mean," when in reality I had no idea what he meant. Needed for what? I knew he had to be on welfare or supported by his family. I even wondered all along who cleaned his house, cared for him, or who visited him besides me. He had never spoken to me about friends, relatives, or anyone. Of course, it was also none of my business.

"I wanted you to know before I left that it's all an illusion. You know the old saying, 'Believe some of what you see and none of what you hear.' However, what was left for you to discover was *seeing* with your *inner eye*, and *hearing* that *silent inner voice.* Once you see this, really see this, you see it all."

"Look, old man, I don't understand everything you say and don't want to go away confused until the next time I see you, so ease up on the heavy stuff. You know I always get a headache after being with you."

The old man broke out of his mystical prophet look and went into his grin and twinkle routine. Somehow, I knew the best part was still to come.

"How long a trip will it be to your family?" I asked.

"It won't be long," he replied, "after all, time is an illusion you know," and he almost fell over laughing.

I could not help but laugh, also, because that expression had somehow significantly affected my life and my seriousness regarding time.

Something else happened that I consciously acknowledged for the first time. I felt a deep sense of loss at the thought that he would be leaving even for an undefined visit. Actually, what I was acknowledging was the fact that I had grown to love this old man, as much as any family member.

As quickly as I felt that emotion, I immediately regained control of myself and started acting like an adult, instead of some teary-eyed child. If he had to leave, he had to leave, and that was that.

"Can I drive you to the bus station or the train station when you decide to leave?"

"No, I'll be able to manage that just fine. Thanks for the offer, though."

"When exactly are you planning to leave?"

"Soon. This will probably be the last time we see each other for a while," he said with finality. "But whether you see me again or not, remember to trust your heart. Any answer that will ever mean anything to you will come from inside of you."

He rose suddenly from his chair and said, "I must be going now. I'll be in constant touch with you."

There was nothing for me to say or do, except shake his hand, as I choked back the tears about to explode in my head, and say goodbye. I turned to walk away and stopped abruptly; turned around and embraced him. We held each other for three long minutes as I cried unashamedly and so did he. And then I found myself on the road back to New Orleans.

Damn that old man. How come I had to get so attached? How could he just up and announce he's leaving, just like that? Then the flood of tears came again.

"Damn that old man, I love him so much and didn't even tell him."

Then it hit me! I don't have his family's address nor does he have mine! How in hell is he going to see me by and by?"

I immediately turned the car around and headed back to La Roche like a bat out of hell. I turned off at the sign to Parkersville in a tailspin and a few minutes later, a left at the silo. After seven or ten minutes of driving down that well-known dusty road, I noticed that I had passed the cornfield some minutes ago, but no La Roche. So I turned around and headed back somewhat cautiously as I retraced my drive from the turnoff. As I approached the cornfield, there was no road leading to the post-Reconstruction house I had grown to know so well.

This is insane, I know I'm not crazy. Just take it easy and think, I said to myself. Go back to the silo and make sure you turned at the right place.

I drove back to the silo and proceeded back along the road; however, no La Roche was in sight. So I proceeded about ten miles further to the next town. It was a bustling town of about 500 people, not like the big city of New Orleans. Country folks were strange; they pretty much kept to themselves and didn't like out-of-town people, especially people asking questions about local residents.

So I went to the little building called "City Hall," which looked more like a rest stop. I politely, very politely, asked the old woman at the desk if she knew of an old man who lived about ten miles down the road going toward New Orleans.

She said, "No," and turned to consider her papers again.

Control, son, I said to myself. Control. "If I'm not mistaken, he lives in the incorporated area called La Roche."

"La what?" she asked.

"La Roche," I said with my impeccable French.

"There's no such place around here."

"But I visited him there on many occasions."

"Then why do you need me?"

"Because the place seems to be gone."

"Gone?"

"Yes, it's not there anymore."

"Maybe it was never there in the first place." Then she looked at me suspiciously and said, "Are you from New Orleans?"

"Oh shit!" I'd better get out of here fast; nothing like answering the questions of a small town country sheriff. I said, "Thanks, I must have surely taken a wrong turn," and I left as quickly as I came.

I drove back to the cornfield for the final time and looked for La Roche and the old man. Nothing, nothing at all. It was like the whole thing had been a dream.

The only vestige of our relationship was the scarecrow there in the cornfield, which seemed to be laughing at me. I parked the car and walked over to it, just to make sure at least it was real and I wasn't totally crazy. Anyway, I learned what I learned and no one could take that away from me, dream or no dream. As I approached the mocking stick figure, I noticed a piece of paper pinned to the soft stuffing. I removed it and read the word *maya*.

Epilogue

Life can be anything you desire it to be; happy, successful, painful, prosperous, contributing, conflicting, harmonious, etc. All that is necessary is to remember that you create every moment of living and that you are totally responsible for every occurrence that you experience. To distinguish that which is illusion from reality is to instantly transform your quality of living and experiencing.

About the Author

Dr. William A. Guillory is president and founder of Innovations Consulting, Inc. He was formerly Chairman and Professor of Chemistry at the University of Utah. He received his B.A. from Dillard University, his Ph.D. from the University of California at Berkeley and was a Postdoctoral Fellow at the Sorbonne in Paris. Dr. Guillory has received numerous prestigious awards, consistently served in advisory capacities, and is the author of several books and more than one hundred scientific and nonscientific articles. He is author of the recent popular book titled *Realizations*. His distinguished awards and appointments include an Alfred P. Sloan Fellowship, Outstanding Educators in America, a Danforth Foundation Associateship, an Alexander von Humbolt Senior Scientist appointment at the University of Frankfurt, a Ralph Metcalfe Chair in Liberal Studies at Marquette University, and the Chancellor's Distinguished Lectureship at the University of California at Berkeley.

Dr. Guillory has taken an intensive and wide-ranging program of study, workshops, and courses in psychology, human relations, and organizational structure. This unique combination of professional training, life experiences, and personal success add a distinctive dimension to his seminar approach and presentation. Dr. Guillory has presented seminars in Europe and Canada, as well as the United States.

Innovations Consulting, Inc.

Innovations Consulting, Inc. believes in the power of the individual. It is from this context that programs are developed to serve businesses, or organizations, and heterogeneous groups.

Other books written by the author are:

Realizations: Personal Empowerment through Self-Awareness.

A two-cassette tape audio workshop of the book *Realizations.*

Rodney, and *Rodney Goes To The Country:* A series of transformational books for children.

You may inquire about the Innovations program offerings or books by writing or calling:

Innovations Consulting, Inc.
1225 E. Fort Union Blvd., #200
Midvale, Utah 84047
(801)561-9002

Books and Products to help establish
The Global Spiritual Awakening

A great shift in consciousness is gaining momentum around the globe. This book is just one of many intended to help in this tremendous effort, the awakening of Mankind. We at Uni★Sun have been privileged to publish a number of books that will contribute significantly to this most important process. Please write for our free catalog.

Uni★Sun
P. O. Box 25421
Kansas City, Missouri 64119
U.S.A.